CONVERSATION STARTERS FOR PARENTS OF TEENS. FIVE MINUTES TO A BETTER RELATIONSHIP.

ADVICE AND QUESTIONS TO ESTABLISH A STRONGER CONNECTION AND ENHANCE COMMUNICATION WITH YOUR TEENAGER.

CECE COLLINS

© Copyright Cece Collins 2021 - All rights reserved.

The content contained within this book may not be reproduced, duplicated, or transmitted without direct written permission from the author or the publisher.

Under no circumstances will any blame or legal responsibility be held against the publisher, or author, for any damages, reparation, or monetary loss due to the information contained within this book. Either directly or indirectly. You are responsible for your own choices, actions, and results.

Legal Notice:

This book is copyright protected. This book is only for personal use. You cannot amend, distribute, sell, use, quote, or paraphrase any part, or the content within this book, without the consent of the author or publisher.

Disclaimer Notice:

Please note the information contained within this document is for educational and entertainment purposes only. All effort has been executed to present accurate, up-to-date, and reliable, complete information. No warranties of any kind are declared or implied. Readers acknowledge that the author is not engaging in the rendering of legal, financial, medical, or professional advice. The content within this book has been derived from various sources. Please consult a licensed professional before attempting any techniques outlined in this book.

By reading this document, the reader agrees that under no circumstances is the author responsible for any losses, direct or indirect, which are incurred as a result of the use of the information contained within this document, including, but not limited to, — errors, omissions, or inaccuracies.

ISBN: 9798523574801

*This book is dedicated to my son.
There isn't a parenting book in the world that could have prepared
me for your wit, charm and mischievous nature.*

Your words have great power. Use them to support and inspire.

— KAREN SALMANSOHN

CONVERSATION STARTERS FOR PARENTS OF TEENS

FIVE MINUTES TO A BETTER RELATIONSHIP.

Advice and Questions to Establish a Stronger Connection and Enhance Communication with your Teenager.

CONTENTS

Introduction — xi

1. Take 5 — 1
2. Teenage Connection — 3
3. Variety is the Spice of Life: Ideas on How to Use this Book — 5
4. Rules of Engagement — 7
5. The Not-So-Secret Language of Teens — 10
6. Conversation Starter Questions — 13

CONCLUSION — 55
Resources — 57
Acknowledgments — 59

INTRODUCTION

You're tired of having a rough relationship with your teen. You want to enjoy better communication and less fighting, but you feel stuck.

Imagine having a helpful resource that provides hundreds of conversation starters with ideas for all kinds of situations. Topics include school, friends, family time, sports or hobbies, and so much more! In addition, some questions can be used as dinner-time games, on long drives home, or as regularly scheduled check-ins. All without ever coming across as nagging --just the right thing at the right time!

This book has been specifically designed for parents or guardians of teens who want better relationships but struggle to find the time or energy in their day-to-day lives to devote hours on end to their child.

I have put together this resource to help you positively engage with your teenager, communicate more and hopefully get to know them a little better. Hence, the relationship becomes more solid and positive. Planned exchanges with your teen will act as a catalyst to reduce intense pent-up emotions that lead to explosive episodes. Communication strengthens relationships which in turn brings forth a more peaceful and happy family environment.

Improved communication will help you bridge the divide between you and your teenager, creating a new, positive bond. This book is based on the premise that two people can have an idea or conversation about anything. Within this resource, parents will find hundreds of questions to engage their children. The design of this book is to spark family conversations. It is a tool that most parents can use without feeling overwhelmed by the task. You can pick out a question and work through one question at a time. I hope this book inspires you to have more frequent conversations with your teenager and that you can become the best parent you can be by having an open and honest dialogue with them.

TAKE 5

"Raising a teenager is hard... But being a teenager is hard too, which is why our kids need someone they trust to lean on, to come to for advice, and to share their lives – the good, the bad, and the ugly. Having a front-row seat in our kids' lives is a far better place to be than sitting on the highest bleacher." (Reynolds 2019)

By consciously deciding to focus on your teenager solely for 5 minutes, you will be amazed at the impact this will have on your relationship. Make eye contact, prioritize that moment over all else for at least 5 minutes, be present for them. Even 5 minutes of one-to-one time with our children is difficult in today's world, if not sometimes impossible to accomplish. Homelife, work schedules and technology, particularly mobile phones, all steal precious time spent engaging with our children. We are busy rushing from one task to another, such as cooking, cleaning, working, and school runs. Add teenage phone or computer use to all of this, and you can see how easy it is to neglect the time and attention they need during a complex and vital stage in their development. People are generally talking on the go and trying to do more than one thing at once. We can miss cues from our children that something is off, and we eventually deal with the fall out of not having observed that there was a problem, resulting in tears and tantrums that could have been avoided.

PRIORITIZE at least five minutes to engage your child in meaningful and fun conversation each day.

HERE ARE five tips that will help you build better communication with your family.

1. Talk about what matters to you and what is going on in your world. This allows people to know how much they matter to you.

2. Keep communication open and transparent; no secrets or surprises, as it can be challenging for teenagers when something noteworthy happens in a family member's life, and they realize it has been hidden from them.

3. Be willing to listen when someone needs support with their thoughts or feelings, even if the response may not immediately ease the person's pain or burden; by doing so, you show that you care about them and their perspective.

4. Don't underestimate the importance of words of kindness. Words of encouragement can keep a person grounded. You've probably heard of the phrase, "A kind word goes a long way," and it is true. A small comment can make a big difference.

5. Move towards each other — physically and emotionally.

TEENAGE CONNECTION

"When your child is little, all you want is for them to play alone in their room for an hour so you can have some peace and quiet. Then they become teenagers, and all you want is for them to come out of their room for an hour and actually talk to you." (Reynolds, 2019)

There is no such thing as a silly question. However, there is such a thing as asking the right question. By raising the right question, it will lead to many more open stretches of conversation. Through regular use of this resource, it will help you achieve a closer relationship with your teenager, if not immediately, at least over time. The more time you spend positively communicating with your child, the more you strengthen your bond and the happier both parent and child become. You will both gain a better understanding of each other. Some questions will prompt random conversations to provide insight into who your teenager is evolving into, but most importantly, it will help improve communication and connection with your teen.

T EENAGERS ARE MATURING INTO ADULTHOOD, and they are discovering who they are and what they want in life. You can help them explore, question, reflect, build confidence through conscious engagement. Building on these smaller moments of positive interactions, you will be amazed at how this will affect your relationship with them. Remember, even 5 minutes one to one time each day can make an enormous difference in your child's life. The most important thing is that your child feels heard, understood, appreciated, respected, and valued by you, which will lead to a stronger bond between both of you. These helpful, creative questions will help that tired brain find ways to reconnect with your teen while also warming your heart as you gain insight into your teen's mind.

VARIETY IS THE SPICE OF LIFE: IDEAS ON HOW TO USE THIS BOOK

"What it's like to have a conversation with a teenager: Parent: "Have a nice day!" Teenager: "Don't tell me how to live my life!"
(Reynolds, 2019)

The questions contained within are to prompt some interesting conversations with your teen, so have fun with it. Before you ask a question, consider your answer to it as your child may be interested in your perspective. These interactions will provide a good teaching opportunity for you. For example, as a parent, if you chose the question, "how do you handle conflict with friends?". What life lesson can you share with your child that will be helpful for them to remember in the future when managing conflict?

1. Keep this book close and use it when the opportunity exists, be proactive in finding opportunities to engage your

teen in meaningful attentive conversation. You aim for 5 minutes with your child, and if it exceeds that, it is a bonus.

2. This can also be used as a family game. Pass the book around the dinner table, and each person gets a chance to choose a question, and the person to ask. This is a great way to keep people at the dinner table socializing after a meal. You can take the game a step further and have five questions to work through. This is a fun game to spark some great conversation.

3. Road trip – the question game, have fun getting to know each other better on long journeys. If you have a long car journey, take turns asking different questions, find a new subject to discuss. The fun part is where the answers take you.

RULES OF ENGAGEMENT

"Adolescence is a period of rapid changes. For example, between the ages of 12 and 17, a parent ages as much as 20 years." –
(Unknown N.D)

If you find yourself parenting a teenager, be forewarned that their moods can change in the blink of an eye. One minute they might seem happy and engaged, and the next, they are passive-aggressively pretending to listen by playing with their hair or staring at their phone while you continue with your concerns. And no matter how much of an attentive parent you may be, it's likely that your teenager will have some explaining to do when it comes to following through on commitments.

Some ways parents can help keep relationships strong is by showing teens attention when necessary, giving positive feedback when possible, and being genuine in all interactions. Many teens have a hard time following through on commitments, but parents can help their children by making sure to follow the seven key rules of engagement. This section outlines these rules and shows how parents can work alongside their teenagers.

1. One way we meet our teenager's needs as parents are by giving them positive attention. I mean full attention with eye contact, at their level, actively listening to what they have to say, reflecting their point, etc. If we give them positive attention, it will build confidence and self-esteem. It's a way of demonstrating that we care and they're significant. Focused attention derives enjoyment and interest in whoever is getting it.

2. Be a thoughtful listener. Make time to engage your child when you are not distracted. Only focus on your child and stay in the conversation. Pay attention to what your child is saying to you. For example, if you are reading a book, listening to music, or watching TV, let your child know that their input is wanted by stopping what you are doing to listen.

3. Give positive feedback when possible. Teenagers are trying to figure a lot out. Let them know when they are on the right track. Look for the positives in them, catch them doing something well each day. Never underestimate the power of positive feedback. During my time working as a Residential Social Worker in a teenage residential assessment facility, I would identify one teen that I observed needed extra attention that day. I would start my shift with 5 pennies in my left pocket. The aim was to move the pennies to my right pocket by the end of my working shift. Every time I had an opportunity to praise the young person or acknowledge effort on their part, I would swap a penny over to the other pocket. I aimed to have all the pennies in the opposite pocket by the end of the shift meaning the teen would have received positive praise at least five times within my shift. The pennies were just a prompt to remind me of my goal to

enhance my relationship with the young person, build their self-esteem, and improve their general behavior.

4. Don't interrupt your child, don't finish their sentences for them and do not answer for them. Instead, be focused on their response to your question. Let them get there on their own time.

5. Pause and take a deep breath if you hear something that triggers you. Teenagers can shock parents at times, depending on how open they are. This interaction is a time for teaching knowledge and values and being honest about expectations, rules, and boundaries. Listen to your child, and this will increase their comfort in telling you what they need to. Never accuse, don't ignore, and don't change the subject when they start sharing something that triggers you.

6. Be genuine and interested. Only 7% of communication is verbal, be aware of what you are portraying with your body language and tone of voice. People know if you are distracted and disinterested in what they have to say. Ask them to tell you more.

7. Follow through if you agree to something to maintain trust with your teenager. Trust is easily broken and hard to get back.

THE NOT-SO-SECRET LANGUAGE OF TEENS

"I'll see your toddler tantrum and raise you, a teen that just had their phone taken away."
(Reynolds, 2019)

Parents can tell a lot of what is going on with their children by reading their body language. You can tell if they're bored, relaxed, defensive, open, closed, and angry, or maybe if they're lying to you. For instance, a relaxed teen will have their arms hanging loosely beside their body. They'll walk with their shoulders hanging slightly, their head is upright and not necessarily focused on anything especially, and you may also see a noticeably relaxed face on your child. Their hands will usually be hanging loose, or they may use them to reinforce what they're saying. Everything about their body will say they're open to communication. Other obvious evidence can be displayed on a teen's face, such as a smile or just a relaxed expression. Once they talk, they will speak with a calm voice and a steady tone. When calm, their forehead looks relaxed and unwrinkled. If you can catch your teen in this general mood, this will be the perfect opportunity to initiate a conversation with the questions.

There is no mistaking the body language of an annoyed and angry teen, but I will touch on this for obvious reasons. You may notice the tight muscles on a child who isn't relaxed, and they may enter the room looking stiff with quick, brisk steps. If they are sitting, the young persons' arms will probably be crossed in front of them. Their hands could also be clenched together or closed. Their shoulders are going to be tight. They may not look you in the eye, and they may keep their head down as they speak. Their voice may be low, and therefore their responses are generally short. This is not the ideal time to engage your child in conversation.

Here are some other body language signs to look out for when communicating with your teen:

Frowning - If your teenager is frowning during a conversation, it could be because they are having trouble understanding something, concentrating on what you're saying, or hearing something confusing them. It could also mean that your teenager is upset about something.

Avoiding eye contact - If your teenager is avoiding eye contact when you are talking to them, they could feel guilty about something, or they may be trying to hide something from you. When teens avoid eye contact, it can also mean that they are feeling embarrassed by what you have asked them or are not interested in the conversation.

Asking questions - Asking questions is a great way to determine if your teenager is open to conversation. If you ask a question and they react by getting quieter, this could mean that they are not willing to participate.

Shifting eyes - If you see that your teenager's eyes are constantly moving, they could be uncomfortable with something you're saying or doing. They may be thinking about something else or having trouble understanding what you are saying.

Rubbing or fidgeting hands - If your teen is constantly rubbing their hands together, it could mean that they're nervous about something that is coming up or a sign of boredom or anxiety.

Closed body language - If you notice that your teenager is slumped over and has their arms crossed, it could mean that your teen feels defensive about something. They may let you know that they don't want to talk by turning away and ignoring you.

Sitting forwards - If your teenager sits forward in their seat when talking to you, it could mean that they are interested in the conversation.

Leaning forward - If your teenager is leaning forward when you are talking to them, it could mean that they are interested in what you are saying.

Smiling at you - Your teenager may be enjoying the conversation, and they will smile when you talk to them. Smiling back at your child is an excellent way of showing that you are interested in what they are saying.

Looking at the floor - When your teenager is looking at the floor while talking to you, it could mean that they are having trouble admitting something to you. On the other hand, it could tell that they are feeling guilty about something.

Head forward - When your teenager is looking at you face to face while talking to you, it could mean that they are interested in what you are saying. This will also be an excellent opportunity for them to tell you something about themselves. So, use your questions to engage them and start the perfect conversation.

CONVERSATION STARTER
QUESTIONS

1. What's the dumbest thing or the funniest thing you've done?

_____

2. If you could travel back in time, what year would you visit? Why?

_____

3. What is one thing you wish you had accomplished by now?

_____

4. WHAT ARE YOUR SIBLINGS' or friends' favorite hobbies?

_____

5. Ever been in a real-life or internet argument? What happened? How did that work out for you? Why?

---

6. What is your favorite book, audiobook, podcast, or movie, and why?

---

7. What's something you find interesting, but people don't usually talk about at school? Have you other friends to talk to about it?

---

8. Do you have a mentor? Who is it, and how do you know that person?

---

9. What are the things you like about living in the country in which we live?

---

10. What do you think is the best way to make money?

---

11. Who is your favorite teacher? Why?

---

12. What is the most significant decision you ever made, and how did you feel about it?

_____

13. Imagine our family is going on a cruise. What would be your dream destination? Why?

_____

14. What does success mean to you?

_____

15. What would you describe as the secret to success?

_____

16. What do you think life is all about?

_____

17. What are you most passionate about in life?

_____

18. Where do you think my priorities are?

_____

19. Where do you think your priorities are?

_____

20. How can you live your best life now?

---

21. How do you cope with sad feelings?

---

22. How do you cope with stress?

---

23. How do you deal with difficult emotions?

---

24. What questions do you have about dating?

---

25. How did high school end up being for you last year?

---

26. What was your favorite day in school so far, and why?

---

27. What was your least favorite day in school so far, and why?

---

28. What impact does social media have on your life?

29. How would you ask a person out? (if you have permission to do so)

30. How can you tell if a person is right for you?

31. If you feel something is wrong in a situation, how can you tell?

32. How do you talk to people whom you do not know well?

33. What do you think are the key elements of cooperation and teamwork?

34. How do you think kids get brave?

35. How can I make things better for you?

36. What do you think I can improve on as a parent?

_____

37. What do you think about the future? Are you hopeful?

_____

38. What famous person would you like to be BFF with and why?

_____

39. What do you think are the most severe problems we will face in the future?

_____

40. How do you feel about coincidences?

_____

41. How can you give yourself that extra self-confidence when you need it?

_____

42. Have you had any excellent friends? Tell me about one of them, what did you like about him or her, why was he or she a good friend?

_____

43. What qualities in a person make a good friend?

44. What were some of the good things that happened today?

45. What are the dreams and goals that you have for yourself?

46. When was the last time you cried, and why?

47. What is your favorite hobby/activity to do alone or with friends or family?

48. Where is your favorite place to go on a day off (that is not home)? Why do you like that place the best?

49. What do you think is the most exciting hobby or activity/experience you could do?

50. Tell me about your best friend. What are the three things you like most about your best friend?

51. What is one thing that you admire about your best friend?

52. Why did you choose your friend to be your best friend?

53. If you could ask your future self some questions about yourself, what would you ask?

54. Who is your favorite TV character, and why?

55. What part of your personality do you admire the most? Why do you admire that part of your personality the most?

56. What things do you like most about our family and why?

57. What things would you like to change about our family and why?

58. What would you want to do forever if you could?

59. If you could travel anywhere in the world, where would you go and why? and with whom?

60. What is your best memory with your sister or brother, and why is this your best memory with them?

61. How important is it to be polite in life (and why)?

62. What are the advantages (and disadvantages) of being polite in life?

63. What is your favorite poem? If it's a movie, what is your favorite quote from that movie?

64. If you could meet one person in history (dead or living), who would it be and why?

65. Tell me about a time when the people around you supported you and helped you. What did they do to support and help you?

66. What do you like the best about school?

67. What do you like least about school? How can we change it to be better?

68. What is the best decision/ best experience you ever had that happened in school? How did you feel about that?

69. Do you want to be an actor? Why or why not?

70. What would you say is your greatest accomplishment so far? Tell me about it.

71. What is something somebody has always told you or some people in your life keep telling you that you should do, but you don't do it? Why don't you?

72. What is something that you were told you shouldn't do and you know you shouldn't? But you do it anyway? Why don't you stop doing it? If someone could help you stop doing it, how would that look?

---

73. Tell me about a time when the people around you have not been there for you at all. What did you think when they didn't support you or help you? What would it take to make amends for this? What made you angry or sad at this time? Why did you feel that way?

---

74. Looking back when you felt unsupported, what do you think made the people around you not support and help you?

---

75. Tell me about a time when someone was mean to you. What do you think happened that made them mean to you? How did they make you feel that day, and why do they make you feel the way they do now?

---

76. What did you want to be when you were younger?

---

77. When have you been the most scared in your life? Where were you and who with and what happened to

make you feel this scared at that time? What was going through your mind at the time? Does this still impact you? How can I help you?

---

78. If you could get something you want for Christmas or any other holiday. What would it be, and why would you like it?

---

79. Do you want to go to college? What course would you like to do? Why do you think you would like this course?

---

80. What do you think is more important, working at something you enjoy every day or in a high-paying job?

---

81. What kind of person do you predict you will become after college and why?

---

82. What book or movie would you like to write or direct or star in and why?

---

83. If your best friend would do something awful (like stealing, lying, cheating, etc. Would you tell them that they shouldn't do that? Why or why not?

84. If you got into trouble because you did something wrong, who would you call to help you? Do you feel like you can come to me, and if so, why, and if not, why? What would it take for you to feel secure to be able to come to me if you got into trouble?

85. We all have opinions about news, politics, celebrities, and the like. Do you have a different view on these topics than other people in your age group?

86. Tell me about the last time you got into trouble. What happened?

87. Tell me about a time when someone helped you out or did something nice for you and why it was so special to you?

88. What is the craziest or funniest thing that has happened to you in your life so far, and how did it make you feel when it happened?

89. Tell me something that would be hard for me to know (like a secret). Why have you never told me before?

90. How important is it to participate in different activities, like sports/music/dance, etc.? What are some of your favorite hobbies?

91. What kind of family life do you like best and why?

92. What is the best thing about living right now?

93. What is the worst thing about living right now?

94. What is your favorite time of the week and why?

95. What makes you feel more confident in life, doing something well or having something that says who you are (like a mobile, latest fashion, etc.)?

96. Tell me about a time when you have had to follow a rule where you disagreed with it at first, but then, later on, you realized that it was for the best.

97. How did you feel when you realized that this was the case?

98. Tell me about a time when you did something wrong or not quite right and how that made you feel.

99. What are some qualities (physical, mental, etc.) that you like about yourself? Why do you like them about yourself?

100. Tell me something that people say to other people all the time at school or on the street. What is hip these days?

101. Tell me something about yourself that other people have never seen or would never guess about you because of how you look or act in different situations.

102. Tell me what you think is the craziest thing I would do when I was younger? Why do you believe that?

---

103. Do you think you are more intelligent than other people your age? If so, in what way?

---

104. I will give you a truce if you tell me a secret that you have never told anyone before, and you need to get it off your chest?

---

105. Who do you want to be in the future? What makes this person special compared to other people?

---

106. What are some of your most memorable dreams, and what do you think they mean?

---

107. How important is it to be with your friends and family during stressful times in life? What is it about being with friends/family during this time that helps you?

---

108. What kind of person do you admire the most (and why)?

---

109. What is the best thing about being alive right now in this world?

---

110. What do you think the best thing about being alive will be in 15 years from now?

---

111. Is there anything in your life that makes no sense and can't be explained by any logic? Why do you think this is so?

---

112. Do you consider yourself a responsible person (i.e., obeying your parents, teachers, etc.)? What things in your life define this responsibility, and why are these the deciding factors?

---

113. What would you rather have, your phone or your computer? What would you rather have than those two things in the world? Why?

---

114. What are three things you are happy about right now?

---

115. What is the best thing that I can do right now to help you be happy?

---

116. What is the worst thing that someone can do right now to make you unhappy?

---

117. When was the last time you did something for the very first time? What was it, and why haven't you done that before?

---

118. If this world was perfect, what would be different about it, and why do you think so?

---

119. Can you ever imagine a world without pain, illness, or suffering? How would that world be different from our world?

---

120. Tell me three things that make you feel most special or different from other people in this world or make you feel unique?

121. What is the most interesting or exciting part of your life?

122. If you could change anything about yourself, what would it be? Why would you change that?

123. What do you want people to remember most about you when they think of you?

124. What is the most exciting thing that has happened to you this month? What do you think made it so enjoyable?

125. What is the funniest dream you ever had?

126. Do you know that you are loved? And how? If not, who would be the best person to prove it to you and why?

127. What are you most grateful for at this time?

128. What is the best idea that you ever had? What happened to make it so good?

129. What is the worst idea you ever had? What impact did this have on you?

130. Have you ever been very angry with someone? If so, who did you get mad at and why?

131. Do you have a time when you have been in a horrible mood with someone, and how did this make you feel? How did you deal with this?

132. What do you think will be the most important invention or contribution in your lifetime (and why)?

133. Tell me about a time when someone did something nice for you without expecting anything in return. How does this make you feel?

134. What scares you the most at this time?

135. What rules do you think are essential to have in the family home? Why do you think these rules are important?

136. What rules do you dislike in the home and why? Do you understand why these rules exist? Why do you think it's important to follow these rules?

137. Tell me about a time when you had to learn something new or a new skill at school, and it felt challenging and frustrating. How did you manage it?

138. What is the most challenging thing you have ever done in your life, and how did you do it and why?

139. What was the most outstanding achievement of your life so far? Do you think this achievement will change in the future?

140. Why is it so cool and fun to be alive right now?

_____

141. Do you think you could tell me something that most people probably don't know about you?

_____

142. Are there any dreams or hopes that you want to accomplish in your life? What action are you taking towards these goals? Can I help in any way?

_____

143. If there was one thing that you would do absolutely anything to achieve, what would it be?

_____

144. Who is an important person in your life who has helped you or perhaps pushed you to be the person that you are today?

_____

145. Who has always been there for you when you needed someone?

_____

146. What is the story of your life? How would you describe it in one sentence?

147. What is something creative that you have done or would like to do?

148. Who do you look up to, and why are they important to your life?

149. When do you feel the most confident? And why do you feel that way at that time? What makes these times special for you?

150. What is something that you feel confident about doing or accomplishing?

151. What is the greatest lesson that you have learned? How has this lesson changed your life? Why do you think this lesson affected your life in the way it did?

152. What do you think people see when they look at you, and why do they feel that way about you (Is there a specific characteristic about you that they like, such as attitude or appearance)?

153. What is your favorite memory growing up? What is your favorite memory that you will have forever? And why is it unique to you?

154. What makes your family important to you, and why does it matter so much to be with them?

155. Who are some of the people in your life who inspire you, and why are they important to who you are today? Why do these people inspire you so much?

156. What are some of the things that make your life worth living right now (such as hobbies, parents, siblings, friends, etc.)? Who makes your life worth living right now?

157. What is something you would like to do but haven't done yet, and why hasn't it been done yet?

158. What do you think of when you picture yourself being married and having children in the future? How do you think they will affect your life, and how will they

impact family and friends?

159. If you have ever been bullied at a school, what type of bullying happened? What did they say or do to you? Who helped you? And how did that help come about?

160. What is the last book you read? And how did you feel about it?

161. What is the most astonishing thing that has happened to you in the last 24 hours?

162. Who are some important people in your life, and why are they important? How would you describe them?

163. What is the most incredible time of your life, and why do you feel that the most incredible time of your life is that moment?

164. If you could go back in time and change something, what would it be, and why would you want to change it?

165. If you had to move away somewhere else, where would it be, and why would you like to move there?

166. What is the most amazing thing that has ever happened to you (such as a trip, a new friendship, getting accepted into college)?

167. What is the most important message you have ever learned, and why have you learned this lesson?

168. Who are some of the happiest people that you know, and why do they seem so happy and joyous? What makes them so happy?

169. What do you think is the key to happiness?

170. What do you think of when you picture yourself three years from now? What kind of person are you, and are you happy about it?

171. How much time have your friends spent with you during the past year, and why is that important to your relationships with them?

172. Why is it essential to be a good friend?

173. If you could not have me for your mom/dad, but you could have any other person, who would it be? Why is that person important to you?

174. What do you think that I am most afraid of, and why is that fear-relevant?

175. How would our family change if we had another child?

176. What is the best thing that I do for you?

177. What is the best thing I could do for you?

178. How can I help make our relationship better?

179. What is the best part of your day and why?

180. What is the hardest part of your day and why?

181. Are there any questions you would like to ask me?

182. Please tell me some of the essential beliefs that you have about the world. How have these essential beliefs about the world affected how you feel about the difficulties you have?

183. Are there things that you like about the way your life is now?

184. Do you believe in things like God, heaven, or the afterlife? What do you think?

185. What is the most important thing to learn about other people, and how would someone know this thing?

186. What is the most important thing to learn about yourself?

187. What would you like to learn about me, and what questions would you like to ask me?

188. Do you think there are things that you do not know and that you will never know?

189. What is the most interesting thing that you have seen lately on social media? Why was it so interesting?

190. Do you feel that Facebook is a good thing? Why or why not? What are your opinions about Facebook?

191. What is the most embarrassing thing that happened to you?

192. What would a day in your life be like for me?

---

193. Would you agree that you are not ready for a relationship, or do you think you are? Why?

---

194. What would be the unique qualities of your potential boyfriend/girlfriend?

---

195. What would you like to know about a prospective boyfriend/girlfriend before agreeing to a date?

---

196. What are important qualities about a person for you to love them?

---

197. What are your feelings towards true love?

---

198. What do you think about marrying when you are older?

---

199. Have you ever thought about having a child later in life?

200. Do you believe in a higher power? If so, do you think they play a role in shaping our day?

201. Is there anything on your mind for which you would like to gain my permission?

202. Is there anything you need to ask me but haven't had the chance or time to ask me?

203. If you were given a gift to do anything you want, what would you do?

204. How are your closest friends feeling at the minute?

205. Can you identify five things that you do well?

206. What's your favorite song? Is it the melody you like? Do you listen to the words of the song? What is the message in it?

207. What is your favorite book? Is it the story or the way it was written that you like?

208. What will your dream house look like? Why?

209. What will your dream car look like? Why?

210. What gives you hope?

211. How does the responsibility you feel for your faith fit with having fun and having your own life?

212. If you wake in the morning in a bad mood, what strategies do you use to help yourself feel better so you can have a good day?

213. Do you believe that God created the world? Why?

214. If you found $5000 in the gutter, what would you do?

215. What have you done that someone else would say you did the wrong thing/ that is not good? Have you learned any lessons from this?

216. What have you done that you have been able to look back on and say that you did the right thing?

217. What are your goals for your life over the next month?

218. What are some skills you have that you would like to share with people around you?

219. What do you think would help family and friends have a better bond with each other?

220. What skills would you like to learn?

---

221. How do you feel when you return home from school?

---

222. How do you feel when you have left home to go to ……….. (fill in the blank)

---

223. How do you feel about yourself after you have accomplished something?

---

224. When do you feel confident and safe the most?

---

225. What would be the best way for someone to make you feel better in the face of a difficult situation? Please tell me the best way to respond to you in such cases.

---

226. How can I be the most help to you?

---

227. What are three things you like to do when you have downtime?

228. What is your proudest moment? Why?

229. What do you think is the best part of life? Why?

230. What do you think is the worst part of your life right now? Why?

231. What is the most crucial thing in your life right now? Why?

232. What changes would you make for the better if you could?

233. Do you have days when you dream about your future? What do you daydream about?

234. What would be the best things for you to do today? Why?

235. What is one thing we could do today that could help make your day a little better? Why?

_____

236. What is one thing that could help make your relationships a lot better?

_____

237. How do you feel about our relationship? Why?

_____

238. What do you think is the best part of this relationship? Why?

_____

239. If you were given $10000, what would you do with it?

_____

240. If you got to be someone else for one day, who would you be? To what extent would you change who you are? Do you see yourself as being similar to that person? Name some of the most admirable characteristics of that person.

_____

241. What are the biggest challenges in your life right now? Why?

_____

242. What are some of the things you would like to do someday?

_____

243. What are the things you would like to change in your life?

_____

244. What are the brightest ideas for making a living that you have come across?

_____

245. What has been the most important thing that has changed your life so far?

_____

246. How would you rate your relationship with me in the past week?

_____

247. How much of a difference has it made in our relationship sometimes when I do something special for you?

_____

248. How would you rate our relationship in the last year?

_____

249. What are the most important things that you have learned about living life?

250. What are the most important things you would want for yourself in the future? Why?

251. What do you want to be like when you are old?

252. What are the most important things you would want to say to people about living life? Why?

253. If you could give your younger self advice, what would you advise?

254. What do you want to see the world most like in the future? Why?

255. What is coming up next that you would like to be involved with?

256. If you could become a different person with another family, where would you live? What would you do? What kind of person do you think you would have turned out to be? Why do you think these things?

---

257. What do you think would be the most difference between you and your brother or sister?

---

258. What is it that interferes with you and your brother/sister enjoying each other?

---

259. Do you have any regrets in your life? If so, have you been crying over this?

---

260. What are the two best things that have ever happened in your life?

---

261. If there was one thing you could warn your younger self about the future, what would you say?

---

262. Do you think aliens exist?

263. Are alcohol and drugs a problem in your school? Can you talk about this?

264. What is the most embarrassing thing that I do as a parent?

265. What is your earliest memory?

266. What would you say is my most annoying habit?

267. What would you wish I would do differently?

268. Do you ever feel jealous of your friends? Why?

269. If you were allowed to get a tattoo, what would you get and where?

270. What is a fun activity we could do together?

271. What class are you learning the least in and why?

272. How would you describe your perfect day?

273. Where is your favorite place to go, and what do you like about it?

274. On a scale of 1-10, how strict do you think I am?

275. What joke never fails to make you laugh?

276. What possession do you cherish the most?

277. What is your biggest worry?

278. What's the best and worst thing about being a teenager?

279. If our family had a theme song, what would it be and why?

280. What are the most important things I have taught you?

281. If you could give an award to anyone within our family, who would you give it to, and what would you provide the award for?

282. If you had a magic wand and could change one thing about our family, what would it be and why?

283. If you could take one animal home from the zoo for the day, what would you pick and why?

284. If you had a superpower like flying or invisibility, would you use it for good? And who would you tell first?

CONCLUSION

"You will teach them to fly, but they will not fly your flight. You will teach them to dream, but they will not dream your dream. You will teach them to live, but they will not live your life. Nevertheless, in every flight, in every life, in every dream, the print of the way you taught them will remain." (Reynolds, 2019)

It is essential to model respectful, genuine, trusting, caring, and open communication with your teenager. If a problem arises, try not to avoid it but rather deal with it gently and promptly. It is recommended that you work collaboratively in resolving conflict with your teen. Collaborative work builds resilience and confidence in your child when a problem arises in the future. Seek support or guidance from extended family or an early intervention support service if you feel burnt out from miscommunication and struggles with your children. It is usual for parents to feel overwhelmed at times. Parenting is the most challenging job out there, and parenting teenagers is in a league of its own with all its complexities, so pat yourself on the back and acknowledge your accomplishments to date. You can't pour from an empty cup, so remember that self-care is critical for parents.

All communication with your teen is a chance to practice emotional intelligence, such as listening, reflection, overcoming challenges, and communication skills. This will prepare them for future situations. Sometimes the best thing that a parent can do for their children is to provide them with a good role model and show them how they should treat others. Parenting teens is not an easy job, and there will be times when you might feel like giving up. Remember the importance of self-care in preparing you to overcome parenting challenges and find peace in parenting your teenagers.

Before I go, I want to leave a heart-warming quote I found for your reflection,

> *"If you look hard enough you might just see the toddler in your teen. Maybe it's the way they watch a scary movie with their mouth slightly open, the way they brush their hair away from their face, how they have to wear their favorite fuzzy socks on a cold winter night or how, even now, they sleep with one hand tucked under their chin the way they did when they were little. Our kids might not be little anymore, but the toddler in them lies just below the surface."*
> (Reynolds, 2019)

I wish you well on your parenting journey. I hope you enjoyed this book and gained a deeper connection with those you love. If you enjoyed this easy read, I would be highly grateful if you took the time to leave a review at your leisure.

RESOURCES

Family Zone. (n.d.). Can we talk? 100 questions your teen might answer. Www.Familyzone.Com. Retrieved June 5, 2021, from https://www.familyzone.com/anz/families/blog/100-questions-for-teens

Magee, E. (2020, October 15). 63 Fun Questions to Get Your Kid Talking. Parents. https://www.parents.com/parenting/better-parenting/advice/questions-every-parent-should-ask-their-kid

Markham, L. (n.d.). Start Dinner Conversations with Your Child. Aha Parenting. Retrieved June 5, 2021, from https://www.ahaparenting.com/parenting-tools/communication/family-discussions

Neurodata Lab. (2018, November 16). Experts Say. . . Is Communication Only 7% Verbal? Truth vs. Marketing. Medium. https://medium.com/@neurodatab/experts-say-is-communication-really-only-7-verbal-truth-vrs-marketing

Norbert Juma, Lead Editor. (2021, February 22). Master quote curator and editor on a mission to inspire. Everyday Power. https://everydaypower.com/teenager-quotes

Reynolds, N. (2019, August 20). 26 Best Quotes About Parenting Teenagers. Raising Teens Today. https://raising-teenstoday.com/26-best-quotes-about-parenting-teenagers

ACKNOWLEDGMENTS

Thank you to my partner and son for the love and support they provide, while juggling challenging roles of their own.

www.ingramcontent.com/pod-product-compliance
Lightning Source LLC
Chambersburg PA
CBHW072106110526
44590CB00018B/3338